P9-ARV-449

BIBLE STORIES TO GROW BY

Christian Herald Books
40 Overlook Drive, Chappaqua, New York 10514

First American edition 1980,
published by the Christian Herald Association
by arrangement with Lion Publishing

Christian Herald Books, Chappaqua, New York 10514

ISBN 0-915684-68-3

Library of Congress Catalog Card No. 80-65436

Printed in Great Britain
by Purnell and Sons Ltd, Paulton

Contents

This book and how to use it

The Lion Book of Bible Stories and Prayers has been designed for practical use at home, in church and at school. Mary Batchelor, who retells the stories and has written or chosen the prayers, is herself a teacher and mother.

This book, like its popular predecessor, *The Lion Book of Children's Prayers*, groups the stories and prayers under themes specially chosen to appeal to children and relate to their own lives and experience. There are some longer stories, but for the most part each double page is complete in itself, with Bible verse, story and prayers.

A feature of the book is its variety. It contains stories familiar and unfamiliar, short and longer. The visual treatment is also varied, with picture-strip, story illustrations and photographs. The drawings are a rich mixture – the work of a number of different artists. They will delight children and readers of all ages.

The book lends itself to family use, day by day at breakfast or bedtime (there are themes for 30 days, and 4 'special days'), or Sunday by Sunday, by parents and children together. It is also a useful source book for teachers at school and Sunday school.

We hope the book will bring pleasure to all who use it and help many new readers to explore and enjoy more fully the treasures of the Bible itself.

Our World - God's World

'Lord, you have made so many things!
How wisely you made them all!
The earth is filled with your creatures.'
From Psalm 104

One day, before the world began . . .

Long, long ago there was no beautiful world.
Only dark, raging seas and empty places.
Then God spoke.

1 'Let there be light!'
God made the day and night.
He made the shining sun.
He made the silver moon and stars.

2 God made the air we breathe,
and the sky, high above.
He made the seaside
– and he made the land.

3 On the land God grew great trees
– and tiny plants.
He made all the growing things
we see around us.

4 God made strange and wonderful
fish to swim in the sea.
It was very quiet in God's world.
No sound but the wind in the trees.

5 Then God made the birds.
The birds built nests in the trees.
The air was full of bird song
and the bright flash of wings.

6 Next God made animals – rabbits, tigers, elephants . . . He made cows to give us milk; dogs and cats to work and play with us.

7 God looked at his world and it was good. 'Now I shall make a man and a woman,' God said. 'They will be my friends and look after the world.'

8 God put the first people, Adam and Eve, in charge of everything. They took great care of God's beautiful new world.

From Genesis 1

God still wants us to look after his world. Every one of us can share in this.

We can sow seeds and grow plants.

We can feed the birds in winter.

We can take care of our pets.

We can keep the town and country tidy.

Can you think of other ways of caring for God's world?

A prayer

Thank you for the world so sweet,
Thank you for the food we eat.
Thank you for the birds that sing,
Thank you, God, for everything.
Amen

When Someone Comes to Stay

'As Jesus and his disciples went on their way, he came to a village where a woman named Martha welcomed him in her home.'

From Luke 10

The visitor who was always welcome

The woman had servants to do the work and – this made her sad – she had no children of her own to look after. So there was plenty of time for looking out of the window.

That was when she first noticed the traveller. He had his cloak wrapped about him as he walked wearily into the little town of Shunem.

'Perhaps he is hungry and has nowhere to go for a meal,' thought the woman. 'We have plenty to eat. I shall invite him here.'

The traveller was pleased. He enjoyed the good dinner and a rest. Before he left, the woman said, 'Call in here whenever you are passing this way.' So the visitor often came to their home and shared their meals.

But the woman was still anxious

about him. She knew that when he came he often stayed a day or two in Shunem. He talked to the people about God and helped them with their worries and problems.

'I wonder where he spends the night,' she thought. 'He probably just sleeps on the ground, with his cloak for a blanket.'

So she said to her husband, 'Our new friend is a good man of God. Let's make him a little room of his own. We can build it on our flat roof.'

Her husband agreed, and soon the woman was busy planning and arranging the new extension. When it was finished she looked at the bare room.

'What will he need to make him comfortable?' she asked herself.

She ordered a bed and a chair and a table from the carpenter. When they came, she arranged the room herself and put a lamp on the table. Then she waited impatiently for their friend's next visit.

When he arrived she took him straight up the stairs to the roof and showed him the room.

'This is for you,' she told him. 'Whenever you come to Shunem to teach us about God you can stay here.'

The dusty, unknown stranger had become a good friend. And God's prophet, Elisha – for that was who it was – had a room of his own and a special welcome at Shunem.

From 2 Kings 4

Prayers

Dear Lord Jesus, thank you for all the friends and visitors who come to our home.
Amen

Dear Lord, please make our home a place where visitors feel welcome. Help us to look after them and make them feel comfortable.
For your sake.
Amen

It's Not Fair!

'Love is patient and kind; it is not jealous.'

From 1 Corinthians 13

Dad's favourite

'Why does Joseph get all the fuss?' Dan grumbled. '*We* are sent off for days at a time to look after Dad's sheep. But Joseph can get up late and take it easy.'

'You won't see *him* doing any hard work. Not while he's wearing that fancy coat Dad gave him,' Asher agreed. 'It's not fair! Why is he always treated better than we are?'

When Joseph began telling them about his strange dreams, none of his brothers wanted to listen.

'Last night I dreamt we were all tying Dad's wheat into sheaves,' Joseph began. '*My* sheaf stood up straight and your sheaves all bowed down to it.'

The brothers turned on him angrily. 'Who do you think you are?' Dan asked. 'You're almost the youngest. So don't think you're going to boss us.'

The other brothers scowled at Joseph and went out without a word. Joseph gave a sigh. None of them seemed to like him or to want to be friends.

A few nights later, Joseph had another of his dreams.

'I dreamt that the sun and the moon and eleven stars were all bowing down to me,' he told his brothers. Simeon gave him a punch. The others told him to keep his dreams to himself in future.

'We're off to Shechem tomorrow, to find fresh pasture for the sheep,' Dan reminded his brothers. 'That'll get us away from Joseph and his stupid dreams.'

The days passed, and the brothers did not return. Their father, Jacob, began to worry.

'Go and make sure that your brothers and the flocks are safe,' he told Joseph.

So Joseph set out, wearing the special coat that his father had given him. By the time he reached Shechem his brothers had gone.

off his special coat, and threw him down the well. Then, ignoring his cries, they sat down to eat their dinner.

'They went on to Dothan,' said a kind passer-by. So Joseph trudged on.

The brothers were resting in the fields when they saw the distant figure. 'Look over there!' shouted Dan. 'Can you see who it is?'

'It's the Dreamer!' exclaimed Simeon. 'I'd know that coat anywhere. Listen lads, now's our chance to get rid of him once and for all. We're miles from home and there's no one to see us. Let's kill Joseph and get rid of the body down this empty well. Then we'll see what becomes of his dreams.'

The others murmured agreement. But Reuben wanted to save Joseph.

'Don't let's kill him,' he said. 'Let's just throw him down the well to teach him a lesson.' Reuben was planning to rescue Joseph as soon as he had the chance, and send him off home.

Before they could say any more, Joseph had arrived. Without a word his brothers got hold of him, ripped

'We can deal with young Joseph later,' they agreed grimly.

As they sat and ate, they saw a long line of camels approaching. 'That must be the spice traders, on their way to Egypt,' one brother said.

'Why not sell Joseph to them?' Judah suggested. 'He'd make a fine slave! We'll get some money – and we won't have to kill our brother.'

Everyone agreed. It seemed the best idea yet. They hauled Joseph out of the well and dragged him to the place where the traders passed.

'He looks a strong, healthy lad,' said the chief trader. 'I'll pay you twenty silver coins.'

The brothers took the money – and the traders took Joseph. 'Now for that fancy coat,' the brothers said, as the long camel train grew small in the distance. 'Let's smear it with goat's blood and take it back to Dad. We can say we found it, and he'll think Joseph was killed by some wild animal.'

When the brothers reached home,

they told their story to Jacob. He could not stop crying.

'I shall never be happy again,' he sobbed. 'Joseph is dead.'

But he was wrong. Joseph had reached Egypt. He was put up for sale in the market-place. And one of the king's officers bought him. Joseph was a slave in a far-off land – all because of his jealous brothers, and his own boasting. But even in Egypt, God was still with him.

From Genesis 37 and 39-47

Prayers

Dear God our Father, help us not to be jealous of others, at home or in school. Help us not to say or do spiteful things because we are jealous. And help us not to mind when others seem to get all the fuss.
For Jesus' sake.
Amen

Dear Father, we thank you that you have no favourites. You love and care for every one of us.
Amen

When I am Frightened

'The Lord is my light and my salvation;
I will fear no one.
The Lord protects me from all danger;
I will never be afraid.'

From Psalm 27

The storm that did as it was told!

Small waves lapped the side of the boat in which Jesus sat talking, close to the shore of the blue lake. It was evening now, and time for the huge crowd of listening people to go home.

Jesus was very tired. For days he had been busy from dawn to dark, curing those who were ill and teaching the crowds.

'Jump into the boat,' Jesus said to his friends, 'and let's cross to the other side of the lake.'

They climbed aboard, took up the oars and began to row. Suddenly the calm lake changed. The wind began to blow, squally and strong. The little boat rocked, then plunged and rose in the rough water. Huge waves broke with a crash over the sides of the boat.

The men rowed with all their strength. But soon they were very frightened. They were fishermen who knew the lake well. They knew how easily these sudden storms

could upset a boat like theirs, plunging them all into the foaming water.

The waves poured into the boat.

In a panic the men shouted for Jesus.

'Look – he's fast asleep!' John cried above the noise of the storm. 'Wake up!' they shouted, shaking Jesus by the shoulder. 'Don't you care that we shall all be drowned?'

Jesus opened his eyes. He stood up in the tossing boat and spoke to the storm.

'Be quiet!' he said to the wind.

'Be still!' he told the waves.

At once the wind died to a whisper. The great waves settled to a gentle rocking. The lake was calm!

Jesus turned to his friends. 'Why are you so frightened?' he asked them. 'Don't you trust me?'

They did not know what to answer. Who could their wonderful friend and master really be? Even the wind and the waves did just as he told them.

From Mark 4

Prayers

Dear Lord Jesus, we thank you that you are stronger than anything we may be frightened of. Help us to know that you are close, keeping us safe when danger seems near.
Amen

Jesus is with me, with me all day,
With me at work and with me at play;
With me at home and wherever I go,
How I should love him
who cares for me so!

Giving Presents

'What can I offer the Lord for all his goodness to me?'

From Psalm 116

The king who had everything

Solomon was a great king. He was very rich. He had a throne of gold and ivory carved with lions. He had a beautiful garden, where monkeys swung from the trees and peacocks strutted proudly. King Solomon had everything.

God had also made him very wise.

Far away, in the land of spices, lived the Queen of Sheba. Travellers brought her news from many lands.

'There is no king as wise and wonderful as Solomon,' they said.

The Queen of Sheba had many questions in her mind. Perhaps King Solomon would be able to answer them?

'Prepare the camels for a long journey,' she said to her servants one day. 'I am going to visit King Solomon. We must take our finest spices – more than he has ever seen – and gold and precious jewels. A great king must have rich presents.'

At last everything was ready. The long camel train set out across the desert to reach King Solomon's palace at Jerusalem. The king welcomed the queen – and told her the answers to all her questions, even the hardest. And the queen gave Solomon all the rich gifts she had brought for him.

From 1 Kings 10

A king in a cottage

Many hundreds of years later, rich travellers set out across the desert again to visit a king. They did not find him in the palace in Jerusalem. Instead, a bright star led them to a poor cottage in Bethlehem. There a mother was nursing her baby son.

The travellers unpacked the saddle-bags strapped to the camels' backs. Then they stooped to go into the small room. There they knelt and worshipped the little king – Jesus.

'We have brought him presents fit for a king,' they told his mother, Mary.

Then in wonder and love they offered him their gifts of gold, sweet-smelling frankincense, and myrrh.

From Matthew 2

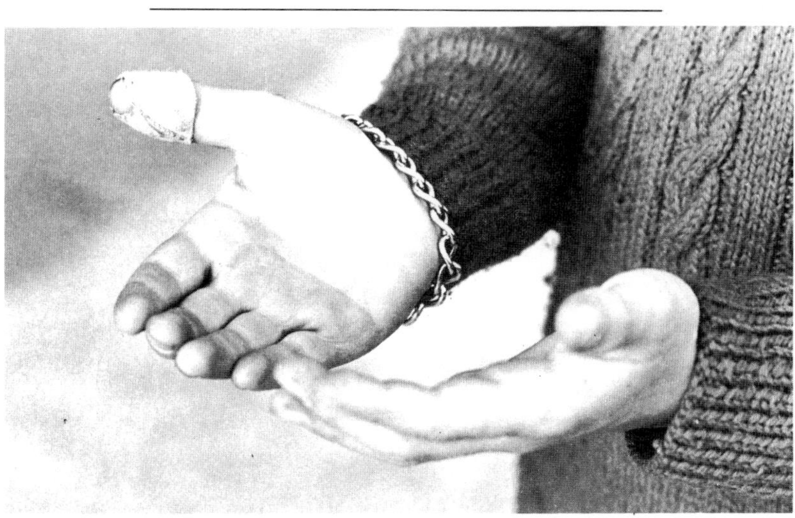

A prayer

The wise may bring their learning,
The rich may bring their wealth,
And some may bring their greatness,
And some their strength and health;
We too would bring our treasures
To offer to the King;
We have no wealth or learning,
What gifts then shall we bring?

We'll bring him hearts that love him.
We'll bring him thankful praise,
And minds for ever striving
To follow in his ways:
And these shall be the treasures
We offer to the King,
And these are gifts that ever
Our grateful hearts may bring.

When Everything is Quiet

'I am listening to what the Lord God is saying.'

From Psalm 85

'Speak, Lord, your servant is listening.'

From 1 Samuel 3

The still, small voice

Elijah was tired. He was frightened. And he was angry.

He was tired because he had been running and walking, running and walking, for mile after mile. He was frightened because wicked Queen Jezebel had sworn to kill him. And all because he stood up for God. He was angry because no one else seemed ready to serve the true God. After all he had done!

When Elijah reached Mount Sinai he found a cave where he could sleep for the night. Then God spoke to him.

'Stand at the top of the mountain,' God said, 'and I will talk to you.'

Elijah got up and went out into the evening air. He stood quite still.

All at once a furious wind blew across the mountain-top. Rocks split open, big boulders hurtled past him and the sound of the wind screamed in his ears. God must surely be in the mighty wind, Elijah thought. But God was not speaking in the wind.

After that, the ground beneath Elijah's feet began to tremble and heave. An earthquake moved the rocks. But God did not speak to Elijah in the great earthquake.

Then Elijah saw the bright flicker of flames. Tongues of fire began to lick the hillsides. Surely God would speak through the bright burning of the fire! But no, God was not in the fire.

At last all was very dark and very still. The wind, the earthquake and the fire had passed. Elijah waited, quiet and still. Then there came the soft whisper of a voice. God was speaking to Elijah in the quietness and silence of the mountain night.

From 1 Kings 19

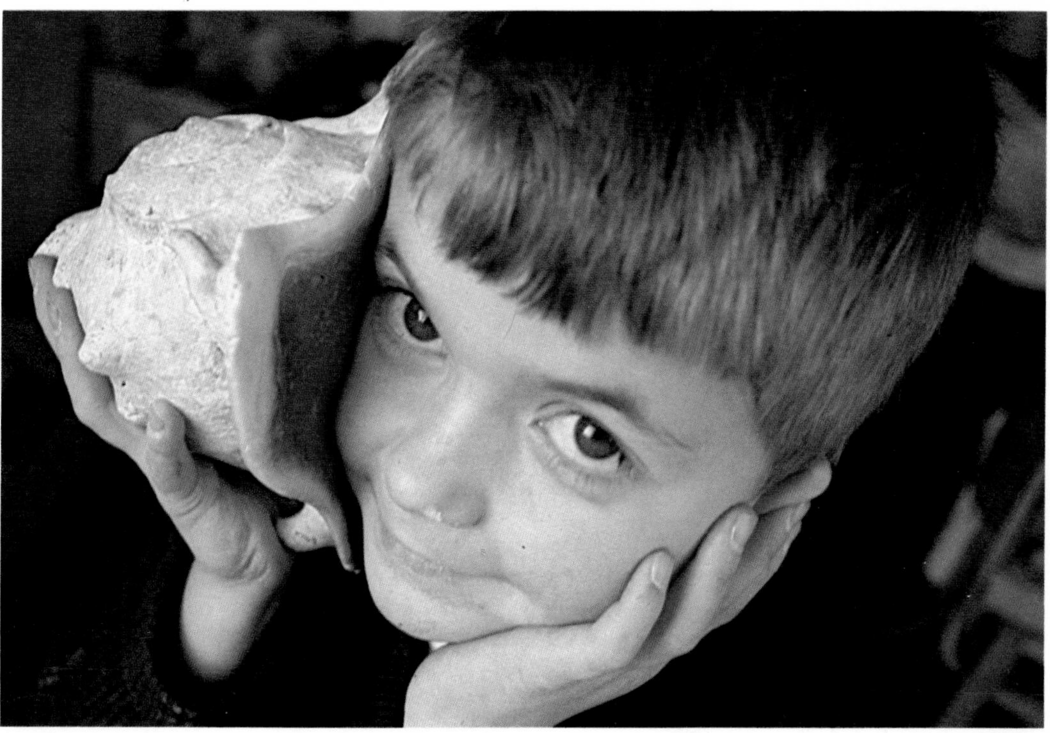

Prayers

Dear Father, thank you for the fun and noise of games, radio and TV, family and school. But thank you, too, for quietness. Thank you for quiet woods, a quiet church, and the quiet of my bed at night. Thank you that I can talk to you best in the quiet.
Amen

Dear Lord, help us to find time to be still and quiet, and to know that you are very close to us.
Amen

Excuses

'Jesus went back with his parents to Nazareth, where he was obedient to them.'

From Luke 2

Jesus said, 'If you love me you will obey my commandments.'

From John 14

The two sons

1 There was once a man who owned a vineyard. He had two strong sons.

2 One day he said to the older boy, 'I want you to help me today.'

3 But his son had made plans of his own. 'No, I don't want to,' he sulked.

4 The moment his Dad had gone, he was sorry. He made up his mind to help.

5 He changed into his old clothes and set off for the vineyard.

6 But his Dad had gone to find the younger son. 'Will *you* help me?'

7 'Of course, Dad,' he said at once. But then he had second thoughts.

8 No need to say anything – he just wouldn't go. He'd stay at home.

When Jesus had finished telling this story he asked his listeners a question. 'Which of the two boys really obeyed his father? The one who said "Yes" and stayed at home, or the one who said "No" but went to help after all?'

What do *you* think?

From Matthew 21

A prayer

Help us Lord Jesus, to obey our parents cheerfully, just as you did. Help us not to whine and grumble, or to make excuses, when we are told what to do. Amen

Rescue

'"Save me Lord," Peter cried. At once Jesus reached out and grabbed hold of him.'

From Matthew 14

Enemy by the seashore

The children paddled in the shallow water while their mothers unpacked the picnic supper. The fathers talked about putting up tents. Everyone was happy.

God had helped his people to escape from the country of Egypt, where the king had kept them as slaves. Now they were on their way to the land God had promised to give them.

At first there was only a little puff of dust in the distance. No one noticed it. Then, one by one, the grown-ups shaded their eyes to look at the horizon. Soon there could be no doubt. Horses were galloping towards them, hard and fast across the desert. More and more came into view.

'It's the Egyptians!' shouted someone. 'They're coming after us.'

'See those chariots and horses!' shouted another.

'Moses!' they wailed. 'What are you going to do? The sea is blocking our way. We can't go forward and we can't go back.'

'It's all your fault, Moses,' moaned one man, 'we were better off as slaves in Egypt. These soldiers will kill us all and our children too.'

Nearer and nearer came the galloping horses. And the people grew more and more frightened. The children stopped playing and clung crying to their mothers' skirts. There was noise and panic everywhere. Then Moses spoke.

'Keep quite still,' he ordered, 'and don't be frightened. God will fight for you. God will rescue you.'

Then God told Moses what to do. 'Tell the people to get ready to go forward,' he ordered. 'Then hold out your stick over the water.'

Moses did as God said and, as the people watched, God made a strong wind blow. It blew the water off the sea of reeds, piling it up to leave a clear path for the people to walk across.

By now it was getting dark. The

Egyptians in their chariots could not see. But God gave light to the Israelites to help them pick their way across.

All night through, the long line of fathers and mothers and children marched. The sheep and goats went with them. The Egyptian chariots began to follow, but their wheels stuck and skidded in the sandy mud. When the last Israelite had crossed over, God again told Moses to hold out his hand over the water.

This time the wind stopped blowing, and the water flowed back over the path. The Egyptian chariots floundered, then sank. The people of Israel never saw them again.

How happy the people were! Moses began to sing a song of thanks to God. Then his sister Miriam joined in, playing her tambourine, and the other women did the same. Soon everyone was singing, playing and dancing their praise to God, who had saved and rescued them.

From Exodus 14

Moses' song of praise to God

'I will sing to the Lord, because he has won a glorious victory;
he has thrown the horses and their riders into the sea.
The Lord is my strong defender;
he is the one who has saved me.
He is my God, and I will praise him,
my father's God, and I will sing about his greatness.
The Lord is a warrior;
the Lord is his name.'

From Exodus 15

Prayers

Our Father, you are the same great God today that you were in Moses' time. Please rescue us from all that frightens us. Keep us from all harm and bring us safely into your heavenly kingdom.
For Jesus Christ's sake.
Amen

Dear Father, we thank you for people of courage down the ages, who have been willing to risk danger or death for those they love and serve.
Amen.

A Family Sunday

'This is the day of the Lord's victory;
let us be happy, let us celebrate!'

From Psalm 118

'I was glad when they said to me, "Let us go to the Lord's house."'

From Psalm 122

Peter's family

'We're back!' called Simon Peter, arriving home from the synagogue service with his brother Andrew. 'I've brought a visitor to dinner.'

Mum could not believe her ears. A visitor, when everything was upside down! She had not been able to go to the synagogue because Gran was so ill. Dinner was nowhere near ready. But before she could say a word they had all trooped into the little living-room.

Then she saw who the visitor was. It was their new friend Jesus. That was different. She began to tell him about her worry at once.

'Please come and see Gran,' they asked Jesus.

Mum led the way to the little bed in the corner where Gran lay tossing. Her forehead was hot and her lips dry. She looked very ill.

Jesus sat down gently beside her. He took her hand in his and helped her to sit up. At once her fever went. She felt quite better. She gave a big smile and got to her feet. Jesus had made her well.

'It's time dinner was ready,' she said, and hurried to set the table and bring in the food. Then she made Jesus sit down and brought him a bowl of water, to wash his hands.

In no time they were enjoying their dinner, eating and laughing together. They talked about the wonderful things that Jesus had said and done in the synagogue that morning. They were all very happy, and Gran was the happiest of them all.

From Mark 1

Hannah's family

Hannah dressed the girls first and made them sit still, so that they wouldn't get dirty again. Then she got the boys ready. At last the whole family set off for their visit to God's house in Shiloh. Elkanah, their Dad, carried the bags but Hannah held one little bundle herself.

As they came near to Shiloh they all grew very excited. Samuel, the eldest of the family, lived here. He helped the old priest Eli to look after God's house and talk to the people who came to worship God there. Samuel's family only saw him once a year when they went to Shiloh for God's special festival.

'How you've grown!' Hannah said as she hugged and kissed her son. Then she opened her parcel and unfolded a new coat that she had made for Samuel. It was a good thing she had made it on the big side. Samuel tried it on. It fitted.

Then they went into God's house together. They thanked God for all his kindness to them since last year. Then they offered their presents to God.

After that it was time for dinner. How they enjoyed it with the family complete. Old Eli was invited, too. As they ate, they shared all the news of the year that had passed.

From 1 Samuel 2

A prayer

We hurry to church in all kinds of weather;
Sunday's the day we can all be together,
Mummies and Daddies and children and Grans,
Even the babies we bring in their prams.

How we all sing, our glad voices raising!
Praise to our God! How happy our praising!
Thank you, dear God, for all that you give us:
Our families and homes, and friends to be with us.

Being Brave

'Be strong, be courageous, all you that hope in the Lord.'

From Psalm 31

'Don't be afraid or discouraged, for I the Lord your God am with you wherever you go.'

From Joshua 1

A drink for the king

King David was hot and thirsty. He took a drink from his soldier's bottle, but the water tasted warm.

'What I'd give for a drink from the well by the gate at Bethlehem!' he said.

He felt homesick as he pictured the little town where he grew up. How many times had he drawn the cool, sparkling water from that well? But Bethlehem was in enemy hands. The Philistines held it. And now David and his men were planning to drive them out and recapture the city.

'Did you hear what the king said?' whispered one of David's most famous soldiers.

'Yes,' answered his friend. 'Why don't we go and get him that drink of water?'

'I'll come with you,' said a third soldier. 'It's well worth the risk, to make our king happy.' So the three brave soldiers set off, sword in hand.

When they reached the Philistine camp they forced their way through to the well by the gate. While two of them held off the Philistine soldiers, the third swiftly drew up some water and filled a bottle. Then, before most of the Philistines knew what was happening, they had broken through the lines again and were running with all their might to the far hill where David and his men were stationed.

Still running, they burst into the king's presence, holding out the water bottle.

'Your majesty,' they panted, 'here is the water you longed for. Drink it!'

But David would not drink.

'My brave men,' he said. 'You risked your lives to bring me this water. I don't deserve such love and loyalty. Only God is worthy of that and he shall have it. I will pour out this water as a gift of love and worship to God, who is King over us all.'

From 2 Samuel 23

Prayers

Lord Jesus, I'm scared. Help me.
I needn't be afraid, because you are with me. You are stronger than anything. You love me. You will take care of me.
Thank you.

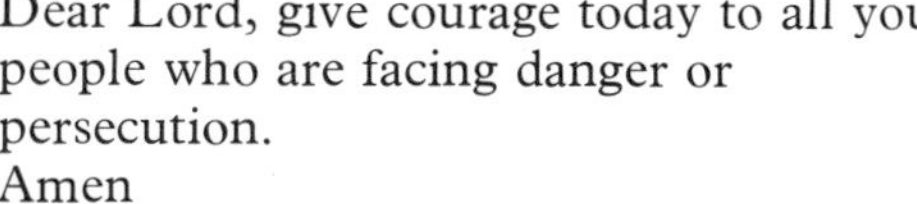

Dear Lord, give courage today to all your people who are facing danger or persecution.
Amen

I'm Hungry!

'God generously gives us everything for our enjoyment.'

From 1 Timothy 6

The best breakfast ever

'I'm hungry,' said Thomas. 'It's a long time since supper last night.' James and John grunted in agreement as they pulled on the oars.

Jesus' friends were very sad. Only a few days before, Jesus had died. Now they were back at work, and some of them had set out in the evening on a fishing expedition. But they hadn't caught a single fish. Now the sky was growing light and morning had come. They were tired and cold as well as hungry.

'Look,' said John. 'We're not the only people about. There's someone over there on the beach.' As he pointed, there came a loud shout across the water.

'Have you caught anything?' asked the man on the shore.

'Nothing!' they shouted back.

'Then throw the net over the right side of the boat,' called the stranger.

Something about the way he spoke made them do as he said.

At once they could feel the net weighed down with shining, darting fishes, big and small.

Then, in a flash, John recognized the stranger.

'It's Jesus,' he said excitedly. 'He's alive again!'

Quick as lightning, Peter slipped off his coat and dived into the water, swimming with all his might towards the shore where Jesus stood waiting. The others dragged the bursting net behind the boat and rowed slowly to land.

There on the beach a little fire was burning. Some fish were cooking on the coals. The air was full of the most delicious smell.

'Bring some more fish,' Jesus said. He knew they were hungry and would want second helpings. John counted the fish they had caught. There were one hundred and fifty-three. Then they sat in a little circle round the fire, drying their wet clothes and warming their hands. Jesus came round to each one in turn and gave them a big helping of sizzling fish and hot bread. It was the best breakfast the friends of Jesus had ever tasted.

From John 21

Prayers

Thank you, Lord Jesus, for making that picnic breakfast for your friends when they were hungry after a night's fishing. We are so glad that you are alive today and that you want us to be your friends. Thank you for sharing in all we do, and for giving us all that we need.
Amen

For health and strength and daily food
we praise your name, O Lord.

Thank you, Jesus, for happy meal times. Thank you for fishermen and farmers, lorry drivers and shop keepers, who work to bring us food.
Thank you for our Mums and Dads, who get our meals ready for us.
Amen

Listen and Learn

'If you listen to advice and are willing to learn, one day you will be wise.'

From Proverbs 19

King Solomon's dream

One day, when Solomon was a young king, he went to offer special prayers and thanks to God. That night God spoke to him in a dream.

'What would you like me to give you, Solomon?' he asked.

'Lord, you have made me king over a great people,' Solomon replied, 'but I am young and don't know the best way to rule. Please give me wisdom, to make the right decisions and rule fairly.'

'I will do as you ask,' God promised. 'You will be wiser than anyone else has ever been, or ever will be. And I will also give you riches and fame.'

Then Solomon woke up.

God kept his promise. Soon King Solomon was famous for his wisdom. He collected and wrote down many wise sayings, to teach other people to be wise. We have some of them in the book of Proverbs.

From 1 Kings 3

Solomon's proverbs

1 'The lazy man turns over in bed. He gets no farther than a door swinging on its hinges.' *Proverbs 26:14*

3 'Singing to a person who is depressed is like taking off his clothes on a cold day.' *Proverbs 25:20*

2 'Gossip is so tasty! How we love to swallow it!' *Proverbs 26:22*

4 'Give a silly answer to a silly question, and the one who asked it will realize that he's not as clever as he thinks.' *Proverbs 26:5*

5 'People who promise things that they never give are like clouds and wind that bring no rain.' *Proverbs 25:14*

6 'Depending on an unreliable person in a crisis is like trying to chew with a loose tooth.' *Proverbs 25:19*

7 'A man away from home is like a bird away from its nest.' *Proverbs 27:8*

8 'You might as well curse your friend as wake him up early in the morning with a loud greeting.' *Proverbs 27:14*

9 'The lazy man stays at home; he says a lion might get him if he goes outside.' *Proverbs 22:13*

10 'Smiling faces make you happy, and good news makes you feel better.' *Proverbs 15:30*

A prayer

Dear Father, please make us wise, to choose and do what is right and good. May we always be ready to learn from others and from your word, the Bible. Help us always to please you.
For Jesus' sake.
Amen

Being Kind

'Our love . . . must be true love, which shows itself in action.'

From 1 John 3

Stuck in the mud

I knew it wasn't really the king's fault. He had wanted to know God's message. And he had promised not to send me back to prison. But the princes and courtiers hated me for telling the people to obey God.

'Jeremiah is saying our city will be captured by the enemy army. He should be put to death,' they told the king. So the king agreed to let them do as they liked with me. I was seized and marched off to the palace.

When they reached the well in the courtyard, they stopped. They put ropes under my arms and lowered me down. The mud walls of the well were slimy. But I guessed there wouldn't be much water at the bottom. The weather was too dry. I landed, just as I expected, in a thick layer of oozing mud.

There was no escape. I could never have climbed those steep, slippery walls – even when I was young and agile. And after months in prison I was thin and weak. As my feet sank down into the mud my spirits sank, too.

A long time seemed to pass. I couldn't move – my feet were stuck fast. I thought I would surely die.

Suddenly I heard a shout from the top.

'Hi, Jeremiah!' The voice sounded friendly.

Peering up through the gloom I could just make out the cheerful face of Ebedmelech, King Zedekiah's African slave.

'We'll soon have you out,' he said. 'As soon as I heard what the princes had done, I went and told the king. He sent us to rescue you.'

A rope came down over the side of the well with something tied to it. As soon as I could reach it, I grabbed hold. It looked like a bundle of rags.

'It's just some old clothes I found in the palace store-room,' Ebedmelech called down. 'Put them under your arms, then the ropes won't hurt when we pull you up.' How kind he was! I put my arms through the loops of the ropes, with a thick padding of rags next to my skin.

'Ready!' I shouted. And Ebedmelech and his friends began to haul me up.

At first the mud sucked me back. Then there was a great squelch – and my feet were free! Up, up I went. I breathed the clean fresh air. I could feel the warmth of the sun.

You can't think how good it was to see Ebedmelech's beaming face and to feel his strong arm helping me onto dry ground! I can tell you I thanked God for that man.

Ebedmelech's courage and kindness saved my life that day.

From Jeremiah 38

A prayer

Jesus' hands were kind hands,
Doing good to all;
Healing pain and sickness,
Blessing children small;
Washing tired feet
And saving those who fall;
Jesus' hands were kind hands,
Doing good to all.

Take my hands, Lord Jesus,
Let them work for you,
Make them strong and gentle,
Kind in all I do;
Let me watch you, Jesus,
Till I'm gentle too,
Till my hands are kind hands,
Quick to work for you.

Friends

'Some friendships do not last but some friends are more loyal than brothers.'

From Proverbs 18

Best friends

Prince Jonathan looked hard at the young man who was talking to his father, King Saul. The shepherd boy's red hair was tousled and his face was flushed. But today David was a great hero. He had killed the enemy's champion, Goliath, and won victory for the people of Israel.

'You are to come and live at my court,' Saul said to him. 'Be one of my soldiers.'

Jonathan was glad. He badly wanted to get to know David. He had liked him at once and knew that they would be friends.

As soon as the boys were on their own, they began to talk. It was just as if they were old friends already.

'I want us to be friends for ever,' Jonathan said. 'Here, take this coat of mine – and this belt – and sword – I want to show you that I mean to be your friend for ever.'

'But I've nothing to give you in return,' David protested.

'I don't want presents,' Jonathan told him, 'only your promise to be my friend too.' David gladly promised.

In the days that followed, the two friends went everywhere together. Jonathan taught David to fire a bow and arrow, and all the ways of life at court. David showed Jonathan where birds' nests were to be found and how to use a shepherd's catapult. Jonathan had never been so happy.

But King Saul, who had once loved David too, began to be jealous of him. Too many people sang David's praises. They thought him a better soldier than the king himself.

'I'm going to kill David,' he told Jonathan one day. Jonathan hurried to find his friend.

'Go away at once,' he warned him. 'Don't come near my father tomorrow. He plans to kill you. Wait for me in our secret place, in the field. I'll bring you news as soon as I can.'

Next day Jonathan began to plead with his father for David.

'Think how loyal and brave he has been,' he reminded Saul. 'He risked his life to kill Goliath. Why ever should you want to kill him?'

'You are right,' Saul admitted, 'I promise not to hurt him.'

For a time all went well. But one day Saul was in a black mood. David was sent for, to play soothing music to cheer the king. In a sudden fury Saul hurled his spear at David. David dodged nimbly aside, then fled from the palace.

'Jonathan,' he asked his friend, 'why should your father want to kill me? What have I done wrong?' They were walking through the fields as usual.

'I will try to make him change his mind again,' Jonathan promised. 'Hide here until I can let you know if it's safe to come back.'

At supper that night Jonathan began to talk about David to the king. But the king flew into a rage.

'At this rate David will be king instead of you,' he shouted. 'How dare you take sides with him against your own father? I'll kill you too!'

Jonathan was very angry. He left the table without eating.

Next morning, very sadly, he went to tell his friend the bad news. They hugged each other and the tears came to their eyes. They knew that David had to go away, perhaps for ever. Although Jonathan was sad to lose his friend, it was more important that David should be safe.

'Never forget our promise to be friends,' he said. 'God will keep us true to each other for ever. May God go with you.'

David was even more upset than Jonathan. He set off, leaving the court, to live in hiding from the angry king. Jonathan went sadly back to the palace.

In the years that followed David had many narrow escapes and exciting adventures. At long last, King Saul was killed in battle, and Jonathan with him. David was king. How he missed his friend and longed to have him with him at court. But Jonathan was dead. Now David had no chance to show him the love and friendship they had promised each other.

'Is there anyone left belonging to Jonathan's family?' he asked his servants.

'There is one,' they replied. 'Jonathan had a son called Mephibosheth. But he's a poor crippled lad. He'll never make a soldier.'

'Bring him to court,' David ordered. So Mephibosheth was carried into David's presence. He could not walk.

'Don't be frightened,' King David said. 'I want to show you the love and kindness that Jonathan and I felt for each other. I will give you back everything that belonged to your father and you shall come and live here at court. You shall have dinner with me every day. You shall be my friend now, for Jonathan's sake.'

From 1 Samuel 18-20; 2 Samuel 9

David's Song for Jonathan

Saul and Jonathan, so wonderful and dear;
together in life, together in death;
swifter than eagles, stronger than lions . . .
The brave soldiers have fallen
they were killed in battle.
Jonathan lies dead in the hills.
I grieve for you, my brother Jonathan;
how dear you were to me!

From 2 Samuel 1

A prayer

Thank you, Lord Jesus, for our friends. Help us to be good friends, not always falling out. Help us to stand up for our friends and not let them down. Help us to make friends with people who have no friends. Thank you for being our best friend.
Amen

I Want!

Jesus said, 'Watch out and guard yourselves from every kind of greed; because a person's true life is not made up of the things he owns, no matter how rich he may be.'

From Luke 12

The man who wanted more

Gehazi looked longingly at the rich silks and gleaming silver coins that General Naaman was offering to his master Elisha.

'Please take them,' repeated Naaman, 'you have cured me of a terrible disease and I want to pay you.'

'No,' said Elisha again. 'I will not take any payment from you. It is God who has cured you, not my skill.'

Naaman nodded slowly, in understanding. 'From now on I shall worship your God too,' he said. Then he set off with his horses and men, back to his own land of Syria.

As the little company disappeared over the hill, Gehazi shook his head in amazement. Elisha must be crazy. How could Elisha refuse such a rich offer of payment? He didn't seem to

care about money or clothes – only teaching people about God.

Then the idea came. Why shouldn't *he* have the silks and silver that Elisha had refused? He could pretend his master had changed his mind. He could say that some poor visitors had arrived, who needed money and clothes.

Without a word to Elisha, Gehazi hurried after Naaman, riding as fast as his donkey would carry him. As soon as Naaman saw him coming, he stopped and waited. When he had heard Gehazi's story, he eagerly insisted on giving him more than he had asked for.

'My servants shall carry the presents to your master's house,' he said.

When they were nearly there, Gehazi sent Naaman's servants back to him. He smuggled the presents into the house. Then he went to see if Elisha needed anything, just as if nothing had happened.

'Where have you been?' Elisha asked.

'Nowhere,' Gehazi lied.

But Elisha was a prophet of God. He knew just what Gehazi had done. He looked at his servant sadly.

'You have been greedy for riches,' he said. 'What really mattered was for Naaman to learn about our God, who gives without asking for payment. Because of what you have done, you will catch the disease that Naaman had. And you will have it till the day you die.'

From 2 Kings 5

Prayers

I am content with what I have
Little be it or much;
And, Lord, contentment still I crave
Because thou savest such.

From The Shepherd Boy's song, The Pilgrim's Progress

Lord, help us to enjoy the things we have and not always to be wanting more. Make us ready to help others, out of love and not for what they may give to us.
Amen

Asking God

'Don't worry about anything, but in all your prayers ask God for what you need, always asking him with a thankful heart.'

From Philippians 4

When Peter cried for help

Peter was scared stiff. It had looked so easy! They had seen Jesus from their boat – and he was walking towards them on the water. So Peter had called out, 'Tell me to come and meet you, Master.'

'Comre on then,' Jesus had called back. Peter climbed eagerly over the side of the boat and, looking straight at Jesus, began to walk towards him.

But, as the rough wind blew, Peter had looked down, and at once his eye caught sight of the rough white crests of the waves beneath his feet. He thought of the deep, deep lake beneath and he felt himself sinking.

'Help!' he shouted above the roar of the wind and waves. 'Save me Lord!'

With one quick move Jesus put out his hand and grabbed Peter. Then he helped him into the boat, safe and sound, and climbed in beside him.

'How little you trust me, Peter,' Jesus said, 'never doubt that I can hear and help you.'

'Jesus, you are wonderful,' said all the friends. 'We believe that you are God's own Son.'

From Matthew 14

The prayer Jesus taught us

Our Father in heaven:
May your holy name be honoured;
may your Kingdom come;
may your will be done on earth as it is in heaven.
Give us today the food we need.
Forgive us the wrongs we have done,
as we forgive the wrongs that
others have done to us.
Do not bring us to hard testing,
but keep us safe from the Evil One.

From Matthew 6

Prayers

Dear Father, thank you for listening to us when we pray. We thank you for happy times. Please be near to help us when we are sad or frightened.
For Jesus' sake.
Amen

O let us feel you very near
When we kneel down to pray
Let us be still that you may send
A message for today.

Brothers and Sisters

Jesus said: 'Whoever does what my Father in heaven wants him to do is my brother, my sister, and my mother.'

From Matthew 12

The two brothers

What a wonderful day it had been! Quiet, shy Andrew was very excited. That very morning he had met Jesus for the first time. Their great friend and teacher, John the Baptist, had pointed Jesus out to them and they had run to catch him up, then stayed to share the day with him.

Andrew thought again about all the wonderful things that Jesus had said. If only his brother had been there to share it all. He must tell him all about it. At once Andrew hurried to the shore to find him.

'Simon!' he called, as he ran towards the boat where his brother was mending the fishing-net. 'We have found the king,' he went on breathlessly. 'The Saviour God promised us has come. His name is Jesus. Come and meet him now.'

Simon looked up in surprise, then he smiled, dropping the net. Together the brothers set off to the place where Jesus was staying. And Andrew introduced Simon Peter to his wonderful new friend.

From John 1

The two sisters

Martha was flustered and worried. Everything must be just right for dinner today. Jesus and his friends were coming. All morning she and her sister Mary had worked hard, but when Jesus arrived there were still things to be done. She turned to tell Mary what to do next.

But Mary had stopped helping. She was sitting listening to what Jesus had to say.

Martha grew more and more hot and bothered. At last she could bear it no longer.

'Jesus,' she interrupted. 'Please tell Mary to come and help. Don't you care that she's left me all the work to do?'

'Martha,' Jesus replied gently. 'Don't worry so much about the meal. There will be plenty without all the extra you are cooking. Mary has made the right choice. Today it is more important to listen to what I have to say than do the housework.'

From Luke 10

Prayers

Dear Lord Jesus, we are glad that you lived in a family and understand the fun and the difficulties of living together. Help us to be loving and generous with our brothers and sisters, to share our good things, and to care for one another. Amen

Lord Jesus taught that his children ought
To forgive one another each day,
And to give and take for his dear sake;
So help us, Lord, we pray:
For it's rough and tumble, rattle and noise,
Mothers and fathers, girls and boys;
Baby in the carry-cot, cat by the stove;
A little bit of quarrelling,
But much more love.

Sad Days

'Listen to my cry for help,
My God and King!'
From Psalm 5

Job's story

1 Long ago there lived a man called Job. He was very rich, with sheep and camels, servants and farm workers.

2 He had a wife and a large family: seven sons and three daughters. He was a good man and he loved God. He was also very happy.

3 One day a servant came running, 'Master!' he cried. 'Raiders came and stole your donkeys and killed your workers.'

4 Before he had finished, another breathless servant arrived. 'Master, lightning struck your sheep and shepherds and killed them all.'

5 A third servant interrupted: 'Master, raiders came and stole your camels and killed your men. I am the only one who escaped.'

6 Up came another servant. 'Master, a sudden storm blew down the house where your family were holding a feast. All your children are dead.'

7 Job was very sad. But he still thanked God for his goodness. Then Job fell ill, with sores all over his body. He was very miserable.

8 Three of Job's friends came to cheer him up. But they only made him feel worse. They told Job God must be angry with him.

9 Then God spoke to Job. 'I am the God who made the earth and the sea. I hold the shining stars in place.'

10 'I send refreshing rain and flashing lightning, frost and ice and gentle dew. Am I not great enough to keep you safe?'

11 'I made and care for all the animals – shy wild deer and prancing horses. Do you think I won't love and look after you, too?'

12 Job still did not understand why his troubles had come. But now he knew he could safely trust God's wise plans.

Prayers

Dear Father, please be close to everyone who is sad or ill, especially children. Help them to remember how great and wise and loving you are.
Amen

When we are happy, full of fun,
Enjoying all the things we've done,
God is with us, God is with us.

When we're puzzled, wondering why
Some days our best friends make us cry,
God is with us, God is with us.

When we are sad and nothing's right,
Although we try with all our might,
God is with us, God is with us.

The Best Book

'Ever since you were a child, you have known the Holy Scriptures, which are able to give you the wisdom that leads to salvation through faith in Christ Jesus.'
From 2 Timothy 3

The man who brought good news

The Queen's Treasurer scratched his head and sighed. He looked out of the carriage in which he was riding, at the bare sandy desert road that stretched ahead. Then, with a frown, he pored again over the new book he had just bought in Jerusalem. It was so hard to understand!

He began reading again, out loud, and he was so intent on what he was doing that he did not notice the stranger who had run alongside his carriage. Then a voice interrupted his reading.

'Do you understand your book?' asked the stranger.

'No, I don't,' the Treasurer replied. 'Can you help? If so, come up here beside me and explain as we go along.'

The stranger climbed into the carriage and sat down.

'This is what my book says, went on the Treasurer: "Like a sheep that is taken to be slaughtered he did not say a word." Now, who is the writer talking about. Himself? Or someone else?' 'No, it's not himself,' said Philip – for that was the newcomer's name. 'The writer of the book is

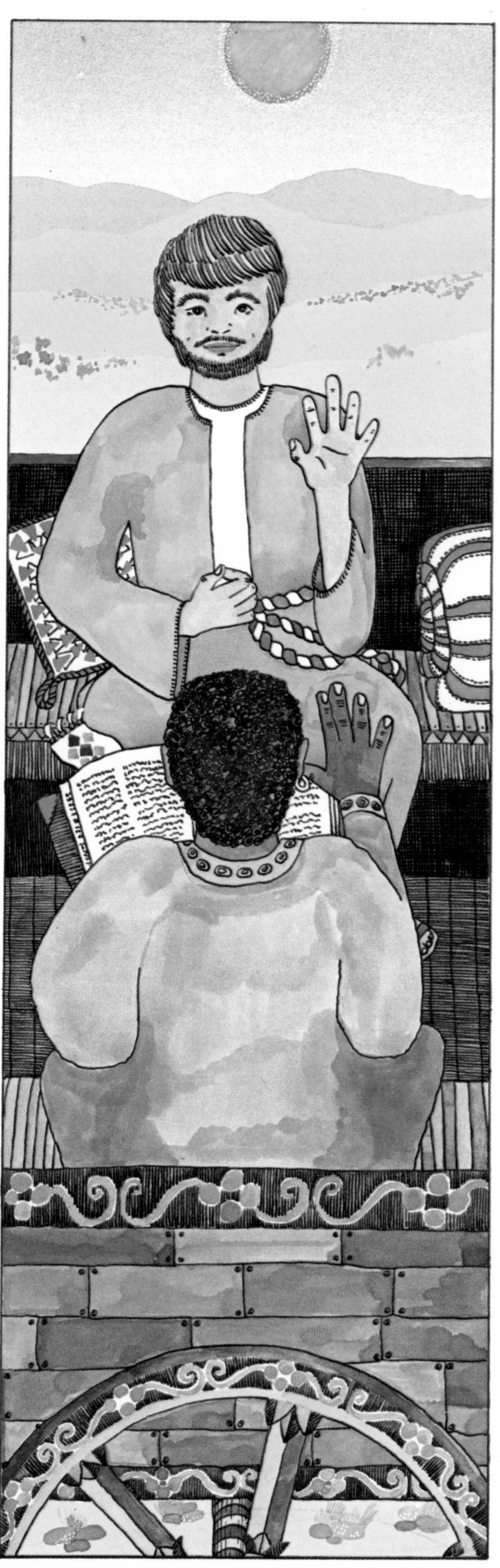

talking about Jesus. Let me tell you about him.'

So Philip told the Ethiopian Treasurer the good news about Jesus, how he had lived and died – and how God had raised him to life again.

'I would like to become a follower of Jesus,' said the Treasurer, when Philip had finished explaining.

'So you may, if you believe with all your heart,' Philip told him.

When Philip said goodbye to his new friend, the Treasurer was full of joy. He drove happily on to his own faraway country to read God's book to his people there and to tell *them* the good news about Jesus.

From Acts 8

Prayers

Thank you, God, for your message to us, written in the Bible. Thank you for the people who first wrote it and for all those who have translated it for us to read in our own languages. Thank you too for those who help us to understand it at school or church or home. Help us to learn about Jesus through reading the Bible, and to love him.
Amen

The best book to read is the Bible;
If we read it every day
It will help us on our way;
The best book to read is the Bible.

Open my eyes, O Lord, to see
Wonderful things in your word for me;
Every word is true and pure,
Every promise is tried and sure;
Lamp to my feet, and light on my way,
Guiding me safely to perfect day.

Alone

'All the disciples left Jesus and ran away.'
From Mark 14

'If God is for us, who can be against us?'
From Romans 8

The boy who killed a giant

David gazed into the clear water of the stream and carefully chose the pebbles. They must be just right – smooth and round. Five would be enough. He put them in his bag and felt for his catapult. He had spent hours practising with it while he took care of his father's sheep. Now he could sling a stone exactly where he wanted it to go. It was better to fight with weapons like these than with a soldier's sword or spear.

He looked across to the hill where King Saul and the Israelite army had set up camp. Then he looked at the hill opposite, where their enemies, the Philistines, were mustered.

Only that morning David had come up from the country to visit his soldier brothers. He was glad now that he had brought his shepherd's sling.

Both armies were lined up ready for battle. But no battle had been fought. Instead, David had seen a lone man come out from the Philistine camp and strut across the valley. What a man! He was enormous. David could hardly believe his eyes. He towered head and shoulders above the servant who carried his shield. And his bronze helmet and armour gleamed in the sunlight. When he spoke, the hills echoed to his mighty voice.

'Come on out and fight me, one of you Israelites!' he thundered. 'If I win, we Philistines shall have won the war. But if your champion wins, you will be the victors.'

'Who is going to fight him?' David had asked the soldiers standing by.

'No one dares,' they had answered. 'Just look at the size and strength of him! None of us would stand a chance against a champion like that.'

'I would fight him,' David said. 'How dare he think he can frighten and conquer the army of God's people?'

Although he was so young, David really seemed to mean what he said. Some of the soldiers who had heard him speak told King Saul. The king was sitting alone and worried in his tent. He sent for David.

'What makes you think that you could fight the Philistine champion and win?' he asked, when David entered the tent. 'You aren't even a trained soldier.'

'No, your majesty,' David answered. 'I'm just a shepherd. But sometimes, when I am taking care of my father's sheep, a lion or a bear carries off one of the lambs. Then I go after it and rescue the lamb. And if the lion turns on me, I kill it. God has helped me defend my sheep, and he will help me defend his people against the enemy.'

'Try my armour on,' the king suggested. 'You must be properly protected.'

But David found the armour far too heavy and uncomfortable. He wasn't used to fighting that way. He would rather rely on his well-tried catapult.

With the pebbles in his bag and the catapult pushed through his belt, David walked alone down the hill and into the valley that lay between the two army camps.

Just at that moment huge Goliath strode out of the Philistine camp, his armour clanking. When he saw the slim young man, armed only with a shepherd's stick and a sling, he could hardly believe his eyes.

'What do you think you are doing, coming to fight me like that?' he roared. 'By my gods, I shall give your body to the crows to eat.'

'You may have sword and spear,' David called back, 'but I come against you in the name of God. And he will give me victory.'

Then David chose one of the smooth pebbles and placed it carefully in the catapult. With practised aim he sent the stone flying through the air. It curved and fell, striking deep into Goliath's forehead and knocking him senseless. Goliath gave one mighty cry and fell to the ground.

Swiftly David ran to him, seized Goliath's own sword and cut off his head.

What a roar of relief and excitement went up from the watching Israelite soldiers!

As for the Philistines, they began to run away, as fast as their legs would carry them.

One boy alone, with God to help him, had brought victory to the whole people of Israel.

From 1 Samuel 17

Prayers

Dear Lord Jesus, you know what it is like to stand all alone against unfriendly and unkind people. Help us when we have to do the same. Thank you for your promise to be with us and help us always.
Amen

Holy Spirit, power of Jesus,
Make us strong to work and fight.
So that when we meet with evil
We may conquer in your might.
Through your name, by your Word,
We are soldiers of the Lord.

Promises

'The Lord your God has given you all the good things that he promised. Every promise he made has been kept; not one has failed.'

From Joshua 23

The day the rain stopped

Rain, rain, rain. Would it never stop?

Noah and his family looked out from the safety of the boat that Noah had made. All they could see was water. What a long time it seemed since God had told them to climb aboard, taking the animals with them.

The floods had come, just as God said. But he had not forgotten about them. At long last the downpour became a steady rain. The rain eased to a drizzle. And then it stopped. A watery sun showed through the clouds and a drying breeze began to blow.

Each day the little family could see the floods going down a bit lower, and a bit lower, until one day the tops of the hills peeped through. Soon the land was dry enough for them to beach the boat and scramble out.

How glad they were to stretch their legs and feel solid ground under their feet!

The first thing Noah did was to build an altar and give God a special thank-you present for saving them from the terrible flood.

Then God spoke to Noah.

'I am going to make a promise that will last for ever,' he said. 'Never again will I send a flood to drown the earth and all its people and animals. Look up into the sky.'

Noah looked up, and there, where the sun was trying to break through the rain clouds, was a beautiful rainbow – red, orange, yellow, green, blue, indigo and violet.

'I have put my bow in the clouds,' God told Noah. 'Whenever you see it in the sky, remember my promise to you and to all people. The rainbow is there as a sign that I will always remember and keep my promise – as long as the earth shall last.'

From Genesis 8 and 9

Prayers

Dear Lord, thank you for the rainbow with its beautiful colours. We love to see it on rainy days. And thank you for always remembering your promise.
Amen

Thank you, God, for all the promises you have made to us in the Bible. Thank you that you keep all your promises. Help us always to keep the promises we make. For Jesus' sake.
Amen

Loving and Forgiving

'Peter came to Jesus and asked, "Lord, if my brother keeps on sinning against me, how many times do I have to forgive him? Seven times?" "No, not seven times," answered Jesus, "but seventy times seven."'

From Matthew 18

The mother who went away

'Where has Mummy gone?' asked little Jezreel. 'Why can't *she* put me to bed?'

His father, Hosea, did not answer his question. 'You must be a big boy and help me with your little sister and brother,' he said.

Next morning, Jezreel's mother had still not come home. So he took the big water-pot and went along the street to the well where the women were getting their water for the day. Two of them were talking.

'Did you know that Gomer has run off again?' one said. 'I don't know how poor Hosea puts up with it. And leaving those three little children, too.'

Then they caught sight of Jezreel and hurriedly began to talk of other things. But Jezreel knew they had been gossiping about his mother. He felt ashamed as well as sad.

Hosea was very sad, too, and hurt and angry that his wife had found someone else to love and had left their happy home. But as the days went by, news of her began to reach their town. People said that her new friends had grown tired of her. She had become so poor she had to sell herself as a slave.

'It serves her right,' Hosea wanted to say. But deep down he still loved Gomer. It made him miserable to know that she was poor and hungry – someone else's servant. He wondered what to do.

Then God spoke to him.

'Go on loving Gomer,' God said. 'Go and find her and bring her home. I know just how you feel. I love my people Israel, just as you love Gomer, even though they do not love or obey me in return.'

So Hosea found someone to mind the children and set off to find Gomer. He had to pay to buy her back from her owner. It took all the money he had, and the rest of the price he had to pay in corn.

Then he brought Gomer back to be his wife again and to look after their children.

'When the people see how much you love and care for Gomer,' God told Hosea, 'they will begin to understand how much I love them, and how much I want them to come back to me.'

From Hosea 1-3

Prayers

Dear Lord, please care for families where the mother or father has left home. Please look after the children and fill the home with your love and peace. Help us all to forgive when others are unkind or hurt us.
Amen

Thank you, Father, for loving us always, even when we are bad, or when we stop loving you. Thank you for forgiving us, and for sending Jesus to bring us back to you.
Amen

23 The New Baby

'Children are a gift from the Lord;
they are a real blessing.'
From Psalm 127

The angel and the baby

Elizabeth looked out of the door for the tenth time. Surely her husband Zechariah would be home soon! She had done all the jobs. The house was clean and tidy.

Elizabeth gave a little sigh as she compared her own neat home with the muddle in her neighbours' houses, where children played and grew up. How she and Zechariah had longed for children of their own! But now they were getting old. They must be thankful that they had each other. God had been good to them. She looked down the street again. Surely that was someone coming, getting nearer every moment.

Yes, here was Zechariah, back home from his temple duties as a priest in Jerusalem. Elizabeth hurried to meet him, calling out to him as he came closer. Zechariah waved but he did not answer her call. And he did not speak as he kissed her.

Elizabeth was puzzled, but Zechariah shook his head so she hurried him into the house without asking questions. He went at once to his writing-tablet and began to write her a message.

'Elizabeth,' he wrote, 'I can't speak. While I was in the Temple I saw an angel of God. You will never guess what news he brought to us. You and I are to have a baby son. I did not believe him – and because of that he told me that I shall not be able to talk until after our son is born.'

Elizabeth did not know whether to laugh or cry for happiness. *She* believed the angel! They had prayed so often for a baby and now God had answered their prayers.

There were busy days ahead for Elizabeth, getting everything ready for the new baby. There was a cot to be made by the village carpenter and baby clothes to sew. At last the day arrived for the baby to be born. All the relations and friends heard the good news.

'God has been so good to us,'

Elizabeth said, cuddling her baby, as they called with little presents and offers of help.

When the baby was a week old, Zechariah and Elizabeth held a special party. All the friends and neighbours came.

'Of course, you'll call the baby Zechariah, after his father,' they said.

But the angel who had brought the news of the baby to Zechariah had also told him what the baby's name was to be.

'He is to be called John,' Elizabeth said firmly.

'What does his father think?' they asked doubtfully.

Zechariah made signs for them to hand him his writing-tablet. 'His name is John,' he wrote.

Then, all at once, Zechariah could speak again. He was full of God's praise. And he told everyone how good God had been in giving them a son. More important still, he told them that John was going to grow up to serve God in a special way. God had chosen him to get everything ready for the coming of the promised king, and to tell everyone that he was coming soon.

From Luke 1

A prayer

Dear Lord Jesus, please bless all
new babies. Help their mothers and
fathers and brothers and sisters to take
great care of them. Thank you for the
happiness they bring.
Amen

Parties and Treats

'All of us should eat and drink and enjoy what we have worked for. It is God's gift.'

From Ecclesiastes 3

'Levi had a big feast in his house for Jesus.'

From Luke 5

A party for Jesus

No one ever invited Matthew to dinner or tea or to a party. Sometimes his neighbours would not speak to him and the children at the end of the street would throw stones or lumps of earth as he hurried to the office.

Matthew had a big house. He was rich. But no one loved him. His job was to collect money from his own people to hand over to the hated Roman rulers. He often demanded extra taxes and kept some for himself.

This particular day began like any other. Matthew sat counting his money. He stopped to write in his big cash book. Through the open door of his little office he could see the lake sparkling in the sun.

There was a crowd of people on the shore. They were laughing and talking with Jesus, the new teacher. Matthew had heard about him. But someone good like that would not want to talk to a cheating tax collector. Matthew began to count once more, the gold coins clinking through his quick fingers.

Suddenly he looked up with a start to see Jesus standing smiling in the doorway.

'Matthew,' Jesus said, 'come with me.' Matthew could not believe his ears. Jesus wanted him.

Coins rolled to the floor. With one stride Matthew left his office for ever. More than anything else he wanted to follow Jesus wherever he went. Even now he could hardly believe that Jesus could love and forgive someone like him.

Good news like that called for a celebration. And that was just what Matthew decided to do. He would give a splendid party. He would invite all the other hated tax collectors. Jesus would be the most important guest.

Matthew sent a message home, telling his servants to prepare the biggest feast of their lives. Then he began to send his invitations.

It was a wonderful party. There was every kind of food and drink. Plates were piled high, and the

servants hurried from guest to guest. There was music and singing.

Then Matthew clapped his hands for quiet. It was time to listen to what Jesus had to say. Matthew wanted everyone to share the good news he had heard. God loved them. Jesus would forgive their selfishness and greed. Jesus could make them happy and good. This was something to celebrate!

From Matthew 9

Prayers

Thank you, Lord Jesus, for parties. Thank you for school parties, for birthday parties and for weddings. Thank you for the lovely food, for sausages and chips, ice-cream and fizzy drinks. Thank you for music and games to play. We are glad that you enjoyed parties when you lived on earth. Please share in our fun, too.
Amen

For a birthday child

Happy, happy birthday!
Happy year begun!
God, who gives us birthdays,
Knows them every one;
God is kind and loving,
He is sure to hear;
So we ask his blessing
For another year.

A Happy Day

'Praise the Lord, all living creatures. Praise the Lord.'

From Psalm 150

The day when everyone sang

The people of Israel had been captives in a far-off land for many years. At last, with the help of a kind king, God brought them back to their own land. When they arrived they found their houses in ruins and God's Temple burnt to the ground. They were very sad. But little by little they began to build their homes again. And one day they made the plans to build a new temple for God.

1 Carpenters and stonemasons began to cut the wood and shape the stones. The people gave money to pay their wages.

2 They gave food and drink and olive oil to pay for cedarwood from Lebanon. The trees were brought by sea to the port of Joppa.

3 When everything was ready, *everyone* who had come back to Jerusalem joined in and began helping to build the Temple.

4 When the foundation was laid, the priests in their special robes blew their trumpets. The Levites clashed their cymbals.

5 Some of the old people cried. They were thinking of the beautiful Temple the enemy soldiers had broken down and burnt.

6 But the young people cheered. Soon everyone shouted and sang for joy. The work on God's Temple had begun.

This is the song the people sang:
'The Lord is good, and his love for Israel is eternal.'

From Ezra 3

Prayers

O Lord! Shout for joy!
O Lord! Shout for joy!

All together shout for joy!
All together shout for joy!

God is good so shout for joy!
God is good so shout for joy!

Let us praise him! Shout for joy!
In our worship, shout for joy!

Clap and sing and shout for joy!
Dance and sing and shout for joy!

Now thank we all our God,
With hearts and hands and voices;
Who wondrous things has done,
In whom his world rejoices;
Who from our mothers' arms,
Has blessed us on our way
With countless gifts of love,
And still is ours today.

Eyes to See

'The Lord has given us eyes to see with (and ears to listen with).'

From Proverbs 20

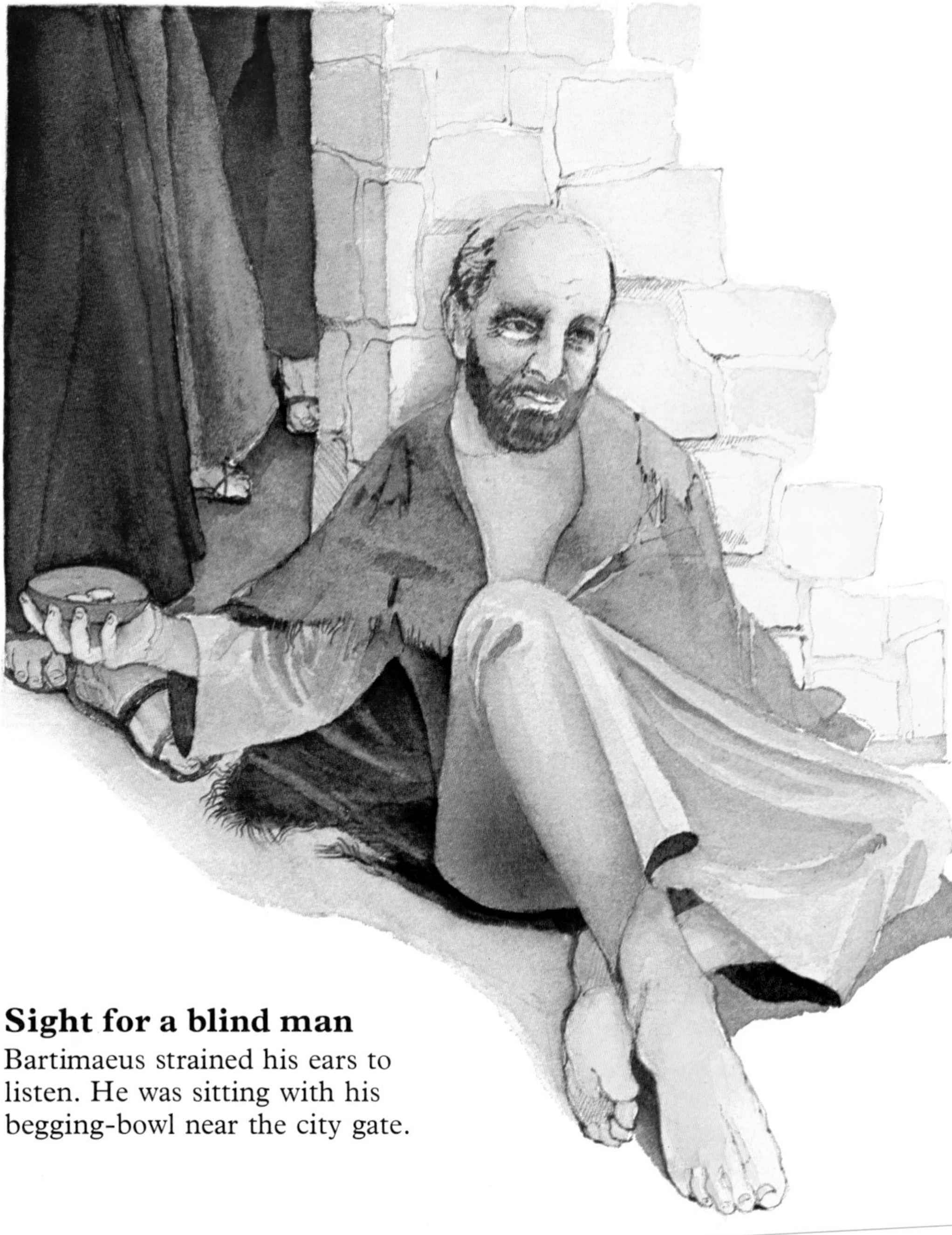

Sight for a blind man

Bartimaeus strained his ears to listen. He was sitting with his begging-bowl near the city gate.

Bartimaeus was used to the sounds of people passing, but today he could hear a big crowd coming near. His ears had to do all the work of ears and eyes, because Bartimaeus had never been able to see.

'What's happening?' he called out. Someone answered, 'Jesus of Nazareth is just leaving Jericho.'

'Then I must stop him, somehow,' Bartimaeus decided. 'I'm sure he could help me.'

So he began to shout with all his might, 'Jesus, God's promised king, help me, have pity on me!'

'Be quiet!' an angry man in the crowd told him.

'Sh!' said several others.

But Bartimaeus took no notice. This was his one chance to meet Jesus. He began calling out again, at the top of his voice.

Suddenly footsteps stopped and Bartimaeus heard a voice say, 'Tell him to come to me.' But Bartimaeus was too surprised to move.

'Go on!' someone urged him and someone else pushed him to his feet. Then Bartimaeus realized that he wasn't dreaming. Jesus had heard and he was calling him.

He threw off his cloak and felt his way forward. Then he heard the voice of Jesus, very close.

'What do you want me to do?' Jesus asked.

'Teacher, I want to be able to see,' he answered eagerly.

'Because of your trust in me you will be able to see,' Jesus promised. And in that instant Bartimaeus found himself gazing into the kind, loving face of Jesus. He did not give his begging-bowl or his tattered cloak another thought. Instead he set off happily, out of the city, following Jesus.

From Matthew 10

The invisible army

Elisha's servant came out of the house. He took a deep breath of the early morning air. Then he looked up at the hills around their town of Dothan – and he saw something that took his breath away.

Enemy soldiers – line upon line of them – were drawn up all round Dothan. Whichever way he looked he saw horses, strong iron chariots and Syrian soldiers. He knew that the enemy wanted to capture his master and now there could surely be no way of escape. He must go back into the house and warn his master.

'Elisha!' he called. 'We are trapped. The Syrians are all around us.'

'Don't be afraid,' Elisha told him. 'There are more fighting for us than for them.'

The servant shook his head. Elisha could say what he liked. There were no Israelite soldiers for miles around, and he knew it.

But Elisha was busy praying. 'Please Lord,' he was saying, 'open this young man's eyes and let him see.'

The servant rubbed his eyes. There was nothing wrong with them. But he looked again towards the hills.

The enemy was still there, but this time he could see that the hills were alive with other horses and chariots. They seemed to shine and blaze with fire.

Then Elisha's servant understood. These were the armies of God himself, sent to protect Elisha and take care of them. They had nothing to be afraid of after all.

From 2 Kings 6

Prayers

Praise to God for things we see,
The growing flower, the waving tree,
Our mother's face, the bright blue sky
Where birds and clouds go floating by,
Praise to God for seeing.

Dear Lord, although we can't see you,
help us to know that you are always near,
especially when we are frightened.
Amen

Let Me Help!

'Then I heard the Lord say, "Whom shall I send? Who shall be our messenger?" I answered, "I will go! Send me!"'

From Isaiah 6

The donkey who carried the King

He was a small donkey, tethered next to his mother in the village street, at the door of the house where their owner lived. He was used to the village children, who patted him as they passed by.

But one day two strange men came up and untied the rope. They began to lead him away – and he felt frightened.

'Hey! What do you think you are doing?' shouted the next-door neighbour.

But the men called back, 'The Master needs the little donkey.' And the neighbour simply nodded and let them go.

The donkey had never been away from his mother before. He pulled back, trembling and braying when he saw the shouting crowds in the busy street ahead.

Just then the man they had called 'Master' came towards him. He stroked the donkey gently and whispered soothing words. Suddenly the donkey didn't feel afraid any more. He stood quite still as the Master climbed onto his back, proud to carry him.

At a word of command he moved slowly forward, picking his way carefully over the cloaks the bystanders spread as a carpet. They had scattered flowering branches to make a royal path. For now the donkey was certain that this was a royal procession. The man on his back was the King.

The crowd roared their welcome and some began to sing.

'Praise God! God bless Jesus who comes in the name of the Lord,' they chanted.

Down the hill into the great city of Jerusalem he carried the king, right to the steps of the gleaming golden Temple. Then, at a word from Jesus, he stopped. His work was done.

Jesus climbed down and the two friends began to lead the donkey back to his mother. How happy he was to have helped the King of kings!

From Matthew 21

Prayers

Dear Lord Jesus, we would like to help you and be useful. Please show us what we can do for you today.
Amen

Hurray for Jesus,
Riding to Jerusalem,
Riding to the city
Up a steep and dusty track.
Hurray for Jesus,
Riding to Jerusalem,
Riding there in triumph
On a little donkey's back.

Wave palms in the air,
Spread your bright cloaks everywhere
And sing, sing, sing.
Shout out: This is great.
Jesus enters through the gate –
Our King.

Children wild with joy –
Every girl and every boy;
They wave, wave, wave.
Only we know why
Christ our King has come to die,
And save.

All God's Creatures

'Praise the Lord from the earth,
sea-monsters and all ocean depths . . .
Praise him . . . all animals, tame and
wild . . . Let them all praise the name
of the Lord!'

From Psalm 148

Small but clever

1 'Ants . . . are weak but they store up their food in the summer.' *Proverbs 30*

2 'You can hold a lizard in your hand, but you can find them in palaces.' *Proverbs 30*

Strange and fierce

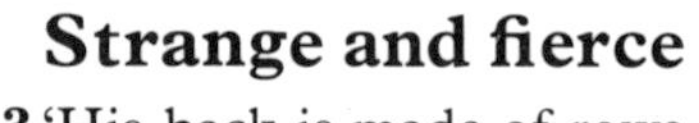

3 'His back is made of rows of shields . . . Light flashes when he sneezes.' *Job 41* (the crocodile)

4 'His bones are as stronge as bronze. He hides among the reeds in the swamp.' *Job 40* (the hippopotamus)

Animals that help us

5 'Cattle know who owns them, and donkeys know where their master feeds them.' *Isaiah 1*

6 God 'made horses so strong and gave them their flowing manes.' *Job 39*

God's plan for the animals

7 'Wolves and sheep will live together.' 'Lions will eat straw as cattle do.' *Isaiah 11*

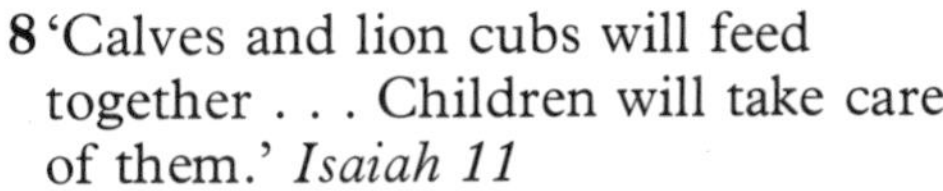

8 'Calves and lion cubs will feed together . . . Children will take care of them.' *Isaiah 11*

A prayer

If I were a wiggly worm,
I'd thank you, Lord, that I could squirm.
And if I were a crocodile,
I'd thank you, Lord, for my big smile.
And if I were a fuzzy wuzzy bear,
I'd thank you, Lord for my
fuzzy wuzzy hair,
but I just thank you, Father,
for making me 'me'.

For you gave me a heart
and you gave me a smile,
You gave me Jesus
and you made me your child,
And I just thank you, Father,
for making me 'me'.

Saying Thank You

'Be thankful.'

From Colossians 3

'How good it is to give thanks to you, O Lord.'

From Psalm 92

The man who said thank you to Jesus

'Jesus! Jesus!' they called. 'Have pity on us, help us!'

Jesus stood quite still to listen to the ten men. His friends stopped, too, but they did not want to get near these men. They had a terrible disease. Because of it they weren't allowed to live at home. They had to keep right away from everyone. But Jesus spoke to them calmly and gently.

'You will be cured of your disease,' he told them. 'Go and see the priest. He will examine you to see if you are really fit.'

Scarcely able to believe their ears, the ten men hobbled off as best they could on their lame feet. As they went, a wonderful thing happened. The sore places all over their bodies healed. Their crippled hands and feet were strong and whole again. They began to laugh and shout and run.

All except one. He stopped short. 'Wait a bit,' he called to the others.

'We never said thank you to Jesus.' But his friends were far too excited to listen. They wanted to see the priest and go home. They wouldn't wait.

The man turned slowly round. Then he began to run back, the way they had just come. When he caught up with Jesus he threw himself down in front of him.

'Thank you – thank you for curing me,' he burst out.

Jesus looked at him for a moment. Then he said, 'There were ten of you. What has happened to the other nine? Are you the only one who remembered to say thank you?'

Then he put a kind hand on the man's shoulder.

'Get up now and be on your way. Your trust in me has made you well again.'

Prayers

Lord Jesus, thank you for everything you have given to us. Thank you for fresh air and food, for families and school, for books and music, for seaside and country. Thank you most of all for showing us the way to God.
Amen

Dear Lord Jesus, when people are kind, help us to remember to say thank you.
Amen

Stand up, clap hands, shout thank you, Lord,
Thank you for the world I'm in.
Stand up, clap hands, shout thank you, Lord,
For happiness and peace within.

I look around and the sun's in the sky,
I look around and I think oh my!
The world is such a wonderful place.
And all because of the Good Lord's grace.

Away from Home

God says, 'Don't be afraid, for I am with you wherever you go.'

From Joshua 1

The dream

'I'll just go as far as that big white rock and then I can go no further,' Jacob thought. His legs ached and his feet were sore as he clambered over the rough stony ground. Every step he took was one step further from home. Jacob felt very unhappy.

His eyes filled with tears as he remembered saying goodbye to his family that morning. His mother had given him a big hug and a kiss and told him to take care. Then she had handed him a little package of food and a bottle of water.

'Go and find my brother, your Uncle Laban,' she said. 'He will give you a home and a job too.'

But now Jacob longed instead to hurry back over the long miles he had walked and be home again. Then he remembered his twin brother Esau and knew he could not go back. Jacob had cheated and robbed Esau – and Esau was so angry that he had threatened to kill Jacob. It was not safe to go home till Esau had cooled down.

Jacob reached the white rock he had noticed in the distance and threw himself down on the hard ground.

After a while he sat up and had a good look round. There was not much to see: a line of hills in the distance, and close at hand just a few scrubby brown bushes and some thin grass. Big stones and boulders lay strewn around.

Now the hot sun was setting. It would soon be night. Jacob unpacked his little parcel of food and hungrily ate the bread his mother had baked. Then he chewed some dried figs and washed it all down with a long drink of water.

It was cold now, and while he had

been eating it had grown nearly dark. Jacob gave a little shiver and pulled his coat more closely to him. He found a good flat stone to make a pillow for his head. Then he lay down and closed his eyes.

'I shall never go to sleep,' he thought. 'I'm too lonely and miserable.' But he was so tired from his long walk that, in spite of the hard ground and the stone pillow, he was soon fast asleep. And as he slept he dreamed.

In his dream he saw a wide steep stairway. It touched the ground near his feet and it stretched up as far as his eyes could see. Up and down the stairway glided bright shining angels. They were busy carrying God's messages and doing God's errands.

At the very top of the stairway stood God himself. And as Jacob gazed in wonder and fear, God came close to him and the dark ground shone bright and clear.

Jacob felt very frightened. He knew that he had done wrong in cheating his brother. Would God be angry with him? Then God spoke to him.

'I will be close to you wherever

you go,' God said, 'however far from your home you may be. One day, this very place where you are sleeping will belong to you and your children and grandchildren. Don't be frightened. I am going to take care of you and bring you safely back after your long journey.'

Jacob woke up with a start. He wasn't alone after all. God was close to him, just as he had been at home, and God's angels were looking after him. Jacob took his stone pillow and stood it on end to mark the place. It would remind him of God's care when at last he came back, as God had said he would. Then Jacob made a promise to worship and serve God all his life.

Feeling braver and happier, Jacob picked up his little pack and set off again on his journey to Uncle Laban's farm.

From Genesis 28

Prayers

Bless all the homeless ones
Near and far away,
And all the sad and lonely ones
Day by day.

And help us to remember them
Always in prayer,
And leave them, heavenly Father,
In your care.

Dear Father, please be close to all children who are far from home tonight. Comfort refugee children and those in hospital. Help us all to remember that wherever we may be you are close to us and your angels are taking care of us. For Jesus' sake.
Amen

Special Days

Christmas

'A Child is born to us!
A son is given to us!
And he will be our ruler.'

From Isaiah 9

The shepherds' story

It was the middle of the night – and cold out in the fields. No warm, comfortable beds for the shepherds. They had to be wide awake in case a hungry wolf came looking for a fat sheep for his supper.

But nothing stirred. They threw down their clubs, yawned and stretched out in front of their camp fire.

Suddenly the dark sky blazed with light and there, in front of them, stood a bright shining angel. The shepherds were so frightened that their legs felt weak and trembling. They could not bear to look at the angel without shading their eyes.

But the angel said, 'Don't be frightened. I've come to bring you good news. A baby has been born tonight – over there in the town. He is your Saviour – Christ the Lord. I will tell you how to find him. Look for a baby lying in a cattle manger.'

Then, as if the light of one angel was not enough, the whole sky grew bright, as angel upon angel came down to sing God's praises.

'Glory to God in the highest!' Their song rang through the clear night.

Then, as suddenly as they had come, the angels disappeared. The shepherds were alone again in the dark and silent night.

They all began to talk at once. 'Come on!' they said excitedly. 'Let's go and find the baby.' And, as fast as they could, they scrambled down the hillside into the sleepy town below.

It did not take them long to find

the cowshed where Joseph and Mary were spending the night. Gently and quietly they tiptoed in, to gaze in wonder at the tiny baby sleeping in the manger.

'We've seen God's angels,' they told Mary. 'They told us that the Saviour we've waited for so long was born here tonight. This baby must be Christ the King.' They knelt in worship before the little baby Jesus. Then, leaving him to sleep, they stole quietly out.

Once they were on their way, they burst out singing, praising God as the angels had done, till the hills echoed to the good news of Christmas.

From Luke 2

Prayers

Sing for the baby at Bethlehem!
Sing for the shepherds who worshipped him!
Sing for the gladness he gave to them
When the great star shone.

Sing for the ox, the ass and the lamb
There in the stable at Bethlehem!
Sing for the flickering candle flame
And the star that shone!

Away in a manger, no crib for a bed,
The little Lord Jesus laid down his sweet head.
The stars in the bright sky looked down where he lay –
The little Lord Jesus asleep on the hay.

Be near me, Lord Jesus; I ask you to stay
Close by me for ever, and love me, I pray.
Bless all the dear children in your tender care,
And fit us for heaven to live with you there.

Easter

'Because of our sins Jesus was handed over to die, and he was raised to life in order to put us right with God.'

From Romans 4

Jesus' last days

Thursday evening
The tramp, tramp of feet disturbed the quiet garden.
A blaze of torchlight lit the dark branches of the trees.
Peter woke with a start.

'Stand up,' Jesus told his friends, 'they are coming to take me prisoner.'

They looked up to see a crowd of police and soldiers with heavy clubs and swords coming towards Jesus.

Peter, now wide awake, took out his own heavy sword and struck at the nearest man.

'Put your sword away,' Jesus told him quietly. 'If I wanted to be rescued I could send for armies of angels. But this is God's plan for me.'

The soldiers stepped forward, seized Jesus and marched him away. Jesus' friends gave one horrified look. Then they took to their heels and ran.

Thursday night
Peter and John were ashamed. They had run away just when Jesus needed them. They made their way to the yard outside the courtroom where Jesus was held prisoner. They could see him through a window. The lawyers fired questions at him. The soldiers slapped him and roughed him up. Jesus' enemies were plotting his death.

Friday morning
A little procession wound its way through the streets of Jerusalem. Roman soldiers went in front, leading Jesus, the prisoner. Jesus' friends followed sadly behind.

When they reached the execution place, outside the city walls, the guards nailed Jesus to the wooden cross by his hands and feet. Then they hauled it upright and waited for him to die.

Friday night

Jesus was dead. His body had been taken down from the cross. His friends gathered round. Where could they take him?

Then Joseph joined them. He was a rich and important man.

'I loved Jesus too,' he said. 'In my garden there is an unused grave, cut into the rock. We can wrap Jesus' body in this sheet and take him there. You can come and see.'

Sunday morning

Panting, Peter ran as fast as he could towards the garden grave. What an extraordinary story those women had told! How could they imagine that Jesus' body had disappeared?

Peter ran fast, but John ran faster. He got there first. But when Peter came up, he pushed past John and went inside the rock grave.

There was the sheet – but there was no sign of Jesus' body. Peter just stood there, puzzled.

'Don't you see?' shouted John. 'Don't you understand? It's just as Jesus promised. He isn't dead. He's alive again.'

Prayers

Dear Lord Jesus, thank you that John was right. Thank you for loving us so much that you died, so that our sins could be forgiven. Thank you for being alive today, to hear us and help us, even though we can't see you. Help us to trust you and love you for ever.
Amen

Jesus died to save me;
Now he lives to keep me;
He will save me,
He will keep me,
If I ask him now.

Whitsun/Pentecost

Jesus said, "I will ask the Father, and he will give you another Helper, who will stay with you for ever. He is the Spirit."'

From John 14

The promise comes true

The friends of Jesus were very sad. Jesus was alive again for ever. But he was going away. He had told them he was going back to God his Father.

'But don't be worried or frightened,' he said. 'I'm not going to leave you on your own. I am sending someone to help you. He will be close to you wherever you are in the world. I am talking about the Spirit of God – my Spirit. Wait here in Jerusalem until God sends him to you.'

It's always hard to wait for something we've been promised. Jesus' friends wondered how his Spirit would come to them, and when he would come. Would he knock on the door, or would an angel announce him?

Then, one morning, as they sat talking and praying together, there was a sudden noise. It was as if a great rushing wind was blowing through the room. Then bright flickers of flame darted from one to the other.

Jesus' Spirit had come! They could not see him. He had no human body as Jesus did. But they knew that he was real and that he was with them. The wind told them of his power. The fire of his presence warmed them.

And they felt like new people now that he was with them. Before, they had been scared and sad – now they felt happy and brave, just as they had when Jesus himself was with them.

They hurried downstairs into the street. There was a great crowd of people outside wondering what all the noise and commotion was about. At once the friends of Jesus began to tell them what had happened. They told them how God had sent Jesus into the world. How he had raised him from death. How God wanted to forgive them.

'The Holy Spirit can be God's

gift to you, too,' Peter told the crowd, 'when you love and trust Jesus, and make him your Saviour and King.'

From Acts 2

Prayers

Spirit of God, unseen as the wind,
Gentle as is the dove;
Teach us the truth and help us believe,
Show us the Saviour's love.

Who can see the great wind blow?
Neither I nor you.
But it blows the clouds along,
Blows the grass and branches strong.
I can feel the great wind blow,
So can all of you.

Who can see God's spirit come?
Neither I nor you.
But he helps us to be strong,
Loving good and fighting wrong.
I can feel God's spirit come,
So can all of you.

Harvest/Thanksgiving

'What can I offer the Lord for all his goodness to me?'

From Psalm 116

The extravagant present

It was a splendid meal. Martha was busy seeing that everyone had enough to eat – especially the most important guest, Jesus.

Suddenly Mary, her sister, got up from the table and went round to where Jesus was sitting. She wanted so much to tell him that she loved him and to thank him for everything he had done for them. At last she had thought what she could do.

Mary had one special possession, which she treasured above everything. It was a bottle of beautiful, costly perfume – from faraway India. Quickly and gladly Mary broke the stopper and poured all the perfume over Jesus' feet. The lovely scent of it filled the whole house.

'What a waste!' muttered Judas. But Jesus understood. And Mary's loving gift made him happy.

From John 12

In Bible days, people brought God presents, to say thank you for his gifts at harvest and for their growing flocks.

Today many of us take harvest gifts to school or church.

We can *say* thank you to God, as well as thanking him with gifts. Here are some verses from the psalms which we can use today:

'The land has produced its harvest;
God, our God, has blessed us.
God has blessed us;
may all people everywhere honour him.'

Psalm 67

'How good it is to give thanks to you, O Lord,
to sing in your honour, O Most High God,
To proclaim your constant love every morning
and your faithfulness every night.'

Psalm 92

'The Lord's unfailing love and mercy still continue,
Fresh as the morning, as sure as the sunrise.'

Lamentations 3

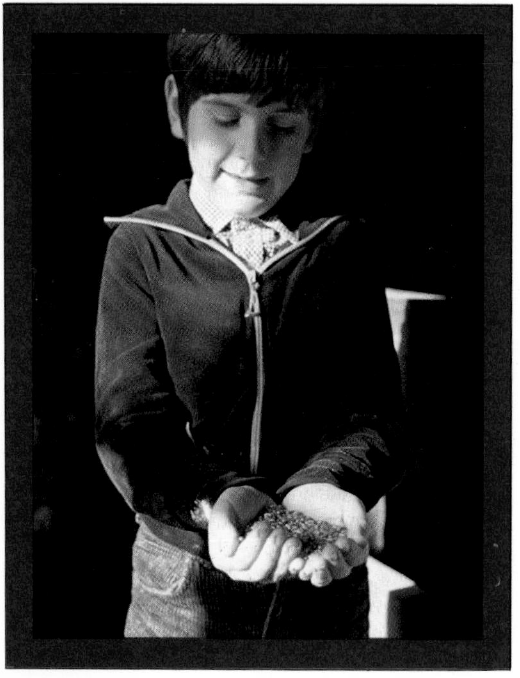

Find a trolley, push it straight
Down the supermarket rows;
  Praise to God who shows his love
  By the food the farmer grows.

Cabbage, carrots, beans or sprouts,
Look and see what Mummy chose;
  Praise to God who shows his love
  By the food the farmer grows.

Peaches, apples, grapefruit, pears,
Reach them standing on your toes!
  Praise to God who shows his love
  By the food the farmer grows.

Cornflakes, sugar, rice and tea,
That's the way the money goes!
  Praise to God who shows his love
  By the food the farmer grows.

Find a trolley, push it straight
Down the supermarket rows;
  Praise to God who shows his love
  By the food the farmer grows.

Prayers

First the seed
And then the grain;
Thank you, God,
For sun and rain.

First the flour
And then the bread;
Thank you, God,
That we are fed.

Thank you, God,
For all your care;
Help us all
To share and share.

We plough the fields and scatter
The good seed on the land,
But it is fed and watered
By God's almighty hand;
He sends the snow in winter,
The warmth to swell the grain,
The breezes and the sunshine,
And soft refreshing rain:
All good gifts around us
Are sent from heaven above;
Then thank the Lord, O thank the Lord,
For all his love.

Acknowledgements

Prayers

All the prayers included in this book are the copyright of Mary Batchelor, with the exception of the following:

Away in a manger: Anon

Bless all the homeless ones: Dorothy E. Baker, from *Praise Him*, Church Information Office, 1959

Find a trolley: Donald H. Hilton, from *New Child Songs*, copyright National Christian Education Council

First the seed: Lilian Cox, from *New Child Songs*, copyright National Christian Education Council

Happy, happy birthday: Florence Hoatson, from *New Child Songs*, copyright National Christian Education Council

Holy Spirit, power of Jesus: E. M. Wyatt and B. J. Ogden, from *Sing to the King*

Hurray for Jesus: Sister Mary Oswin, from *Sing Children of the Day*, copyright Geoffrey Chapman, a division of Cassell Ltd.

If I were a wiggly worm: Brian Howard, from *The Butterfly Song*, copyright Celebration Services (International) Ltd.

Jesus died to save me: George Everard, from *CSSM Chorus Book*, Scripture Union

Jesus' hands were kind hands: Margaret Cropper

Jesus is with me: Basil M. Taylor, from *CSSM Chorus Book*, Scripture Union

Lord Jesus, I'm scared: from *Family Prayers*, Scripture Union, 1974

Lord Jesus taught: Margaret Rose, from *The Morning Cockerel*, Granada Publishing Ltd.

Now thank we all our God: Martin Rinkart, translated by Catherine Winkworth

O let us feel you very near: from *Praise Him*, Church Information Office, 1959

O Lord! Shout for joy: Peter D. Smith, from *Partners in Praise*, copyright Stainer and Bell Ltd.

Open my eyes; O Lord: E. H. Swinstead, from *CSSM Chorus Book*, Scripture Union

Praise to God for things we see: Maria Penstone

Sing for the baby at Bethlehem: M. J. Martyn, from *New Child Songs*, copyright National Christian Education Council

Spirit of God, unseen as the wind: Margaret Old, by permission of Scripture Union from *Sing to God* obtainable from Scripture Union

Thank you for the world so sweet: E. Rutter Leatham

The best book to read: P. Bilhorne, from *CSSM Chorus Book*, Scripture Union

The wise may bring their learning: Anon

We hurry to church: Dorothy R. Wilton, from *New Child Songs*, copyright National Christian Education Council

We plough the fields: M. Claudius, translated by J. M. Campbell

When we are happy: Peter Tongeman, from *New Child Songs*, copyright National Christian Education Council

Who can see the great wind blow: Margaret Cropper

Every effort has been made to trace and contact copyright owners. If there are any inadvertent omissions in the acknowledgements we apologize to those concerned.

Photographs

Lion Publishing, Jon Willcocks: cover, endpapers, facing 'How to use this book', 10, 14, 23, 29, Easter (*photo of chick taken at Rivervale Hatcheries, Chearsley*), Whitsun/Pentecost

Jean-Luc Ray: 2, 3, 5, 11, 13, 16, 20, 26, 30

Barnaby's Picture Library: B. Neeley, 4

Henry Grant: 6, 22

John Cleare: 8

Paul Kay: Harvest/Thanksgiving

Ron Oulds: 27